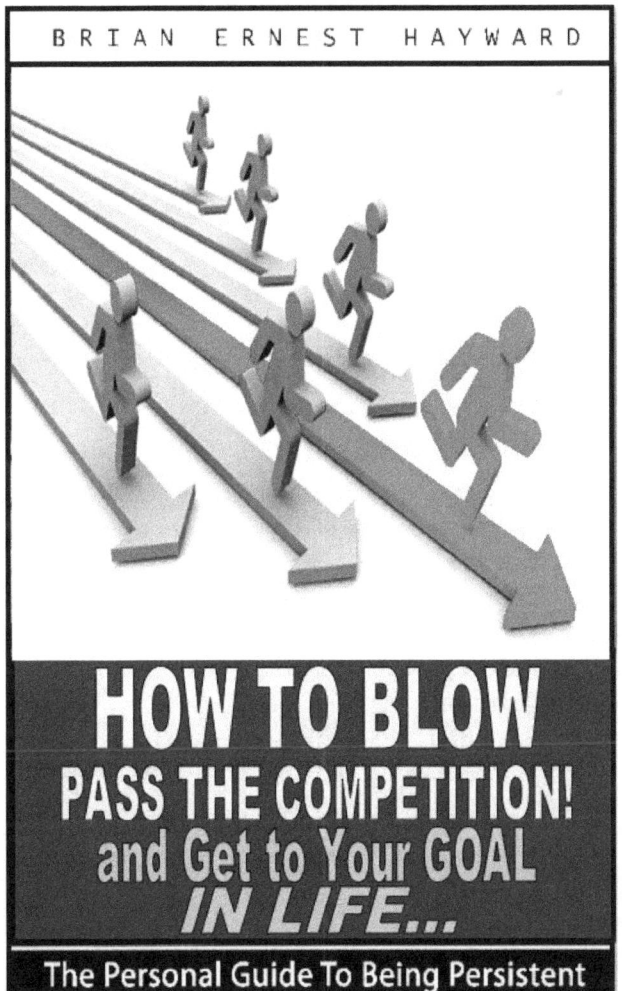

Copyright © 2024 by Brian Ernest Hayward and Published by Brian Hayward for Hayward House Publishing Published by Hayward House and Big Book Box A Member of the Brian Hayward Group All rights reserved. No part of this publication may be reproduced, stored in a retrieval system, or transmitted, in any form or by any means, electronic, mechanical, photocopying, recording, or otherwise, without the prior written permission of the publisher. For information and inquiries , address Hayward House publishing and Hayward Press, Savannah, Ga 31405, Library of Congress Cataloging-in-Publication Data. Hayward, Brian. TITLE=In Jesus Mighty Name Series, Journal WRITING for success in your life / Brian Hayward. p. cm.

PAPERBACK EDITION

ISBN:9798333006608
Imprint:
Independently published

Self-control. 2. Self-management (Psychology) 3. Success. 4. Success in business. Big Book Box Press books are available at special discounts for bulk purchases in the U.S. by

corporations, institutions, and other organizations . For more information, please contact the Special Markets Department at the Big Book Box Books Group, or visit us at https://www.amazon.com/Brian-Ernest-Hayward/e/B06XT464NM

AUTHOR INTRODUCTION

I was taught by my teacher, Pastor Bill Winston, this prayer. This prayer has served me well, and in due time it will serve you well. Father  I come before you in Jesus name, thank you for the anointing that's on me and these lips of clay. I know that because of your blessing, I speak this word today with excellency, accuracy, and boldness.

AUTHOR BIOGRAPHY

I thank you for thinking through my mind and speaking through my lips and this word will come forth unhindered, and unchecked by any outside force. Now I give you the praise for it and I fully expect signs, wonders, and miracles to confirm your word preached in Jesus name, Amen! This is a book about the "new creation" God has made me through Christ Jesus. Be inspired as you read toward greatness and achievement.Brian Ernest Hayward is a passionate Author and Inspirational Speaker, internationally known for his unwavering dedication to creating positive change through the power of words. From religious and success books, to adult coloring books and artist HOW-TO BOOKS, his writings touch on over 400 different subjects. Today, all of Brian's publications are sold worldwide across multiple formats (Paperback, Kindle, and Large Print) and are translated into 21 different languages. He has also participated in over 100 speaking engagements spanning over 38 states.

Table Of Contents

Introduction — 7

Chapter 1: Setting Clear and Achievable Goals in Order to Blow Past the Competition — 12

Chapter 2: Strategic Planning for Success and Blowing Past the Competition — 17

Chapter 3: Building Momentum and Gaining a Burst of Energy — 21

Chapter 4: Innovation and Creativity in Outperforming Competitors — 24

Chapter 5: Leveraging Your Unique Strengths and Blowing Past the Competition — 27

Chapter 6: Overcoming Obstacles, Blowing Past the Competition, and Adapting to Change — 30

Chapter 7: Maintaining Your Lead, Blowing Past the Competition, and Sustaining Success ... 38

Chapter 8: The Psychological Benefits of Persistence and Blowing Past the Competition ... 46

Chapter 9: Inspiring Others, Blow Past the Competition, and Leading by Example ... 53

Chapter 10: Reflecting on Your Journey, Blow Past the Competition, and Future Planning ... 59

Persistence Conclusion ... 66

NOTES... 127

NOTES... 128

Bibliography ... 131

How To Blow Pass the Competition and Get to Your Goal in Life (A Personal Guide to Being Persistent)

Introduction

Definition of "Blow Pass the Competition"

Achieving success and standing out in any field requires more than simply challenging work. The phrase "Blow Past the Competition"  encapsulates the essence of surpassing rivals and reaching unparalleled heights. It involves momentum, defeating competition, and consistently outperforming peers. Understanding these concepts is crucial for anyone aiming to achieve significant goals.

Burst of Momentum

The burst of momentum is akin to a sudden surge of energy that propels you forward. It is that critical push that transforms effort into tangible results. This momentum is not just about physical speed but also about strategic acceleration in your endeavors. When you harness this momentum, you move swiftly past competitors who may be bogged down by routine or lack of innovation.

Defeating the Competition

Defeating the competition is not about winning a battle and maintaining a continuous edge. It involves a strategic approach to identifying your competitors' weaknesses and leveraging your strengths to stay ahead. This requires a keen understanding of the market, constant innovation, and an unwavering commitment to excellence.

Outperforming Peers

Outperforming peers means consistently achieving better outcomes compared to those  around you. This involves setting higher standards for yourself, continuously improving your skills, and staying updated with industry trends. It is about creating a personal brand synonymous with excellence and reliability.

Importance of Persistence

Persistence is the cornerstone of long-term success. It is the force that drives individuals to keep pushing forward despite obstacles and setbacks. Without persistence, even the most talented individuals can falter. Let us delve into why persistence is indispensable for achieving and maintaining success.

Long-Term Success

Long-term success is not an overnight phenomenon. It requires sustained effort over extended periods. Persistence helps maintain focus and dedication, allowing you to build on your successes incrementally. It is about playing the long game and understanding that achievement comes from continuous effort and improvement.

Overcoming Obstacles

Life is fraught with challenges, and the path to success is seldom smooth. Persistence equips you with the resilience to navigate these obstacles. It fosters a mindset that views  challenges as opportunities for growth rather than insurmountable barriers. Overcoming obstacles through persistence builds character and prepares you for even more significant challenges.

Unique Insights

Persistence offers unique insights that are not accessible to those who give up easily. It teaches you the value of patience, the importance of incremental progress, and the power of unwavering determination. These insights are invaluable in personal and professional life, providing a framework for achieving sustained success.

The Paradoxes of Persistence

While crucial, persistence is a paradoxical trait. It is empowering and demanding, offering immense rewards and requiring significant sacrifices. Understanding these paradoxes is essential for leveraging persistence effectively.

Empowering and Demanding

Persistence empowers you by instilling a sense of control over your destiny. However, it also demands continuous effort and resilience. Balancing these aspects is critical to maintaining a persistent attitude without succumbing to burnout.

Steadfastness vs. Flexibility

Another paradox of persistence is the need to balance steadfastness with flexibility. While staying committed to your goals is essential, adapting your strategies to change circumstances is equally important. This dynamic balance is what distinguishes effective persistence from mere stubbornness.

Rewards vs. Sacrifices

The rewards of persistence are immense, ranging from personal growth to professional success. However, these rewards often come at the cost of sacrifices such as time, comfort, and immediate gratification. Understanding and accepting these trade-offs is vital for staying persistent overall.

Chapter 1: Setting Clear and Achievable Goals in Order to Blow Past the Competition

Importance of Goal Setting

Setting clear and achievable goals is the first step in blowing past the competition. Goals provide direction and focus, guiding your efforts and helping you stay motivated. Without clear goals, your efforts can become scattered and ineffective.

Direction and Focus

Goals act as a compass, providing a sense of direction and focus. They help you channel your  energy and resources toward specific outcomes, making your efforts more efficient and effective. Clear goals prevent you from wandering aimlessly and ensure your actions contribute to your larger objectives.

Motivation

Goals are powerful sources of motivation. They give you something to strive for and provide a sense of purpose. Setting and achieving goals creates a positive feedback loop, where each success fuels further motivation and commitment.

SMART Goals Framework

The SMART goals framework is widely used to set clear and achievable goals. It stands for Specific, Measurable, Achievable, Relevant, and Time-Bound. This framework ensures that your goals are well-defined and realistic.

Specific

A specific goal clearly defines what you want to achieve. It answers the questions of who, what, where, when, and why. Specific goals leave no room for ambiguity, making planning and executing the necessary actions more accessible and measurable.

Measurable

Measurable goals include criteria for tracking progress. This allows you to assess whether you are moving towards your goal and adjust if necessary. Measurable goals provide a clear benchmark for success and help you stay accountable.

Achievable

Achievable goals are realistic and attainable. They consider your current abilities and resources, ensuring your goals are challenging yet within reach. Setting achievable goals prevents frustration and encourages steady progress.

Relevant

Relevant goals align with your broader objectives. They are meaningful, ensuring your efforts contribute to your vision. Relevant goals keep you focused on what genuinely matters and prevent you from getting sidetracked.

Time-Bound

Time-bound goals have a clear deadline. This creates a sense of urgency and helps you prioritize your actions. Time-bound goals ensure that you stay on track and maintain a consistent pace towards achieving your objectives.

Creating a Roadmap

A roadmap breaks down your goals into manageable tasks and provides a clear path. It helps you progress and adjust as needed.

Breaking Down Goals

Breaking down your goals into smaller ones makes them more manageable and less overwhelming. This approach lets you focus on one step at a time, gradually building momentum and achieving incremental progress.

Tracking Progress

Tracking your progress is crucial for staying motivated and making informed decisions. Regularly reviewing your achievements and setbacks helps you stay on course and adjust your strategies as needed. A clear roadmap provides a structured way to monitor your progress and celebrate your successes.

Chapter 2: Strategic Planning for Success and Blowing Past the Competition

Developing a Strategic Plan

Strategic planning is essential for turning your goals into reality. It involves identifying opportunities, anticipating challenges, and developing a clear action plan.

Identifying Opportunities

Spotting key opportunities for advancement is a critical component of strategic planning. This  involves staying informed about industry trends, market conditions, and emerging technologies. Identifying opportunities allows you to position yourself advantageously and capitalize on favorable conditions.

Anticipating Challenges

Preparing for potential obstacles and setbacks is equally essential. Anticipating challenges allows you to develop contingency plans and respond proactively. This foresight ensures you are not caught off guard and can maintain momentum even when faced with difficulties.

Leveraging Resources

Leveraging available resources effectively can significantly enhance your chances of success. This includes utilizing tools and technology and adding a solid support network.

Utilizing Tools and Technology

Making the most available tools and technology can streamline your efforts and increase efficiency. This involves staying updated with the latest advancements and incorporating them into your workflow. Leveraging technology can give you a competitive edge and improve your overall performance.

Building a Support Network

Engaging mentors, colleagues, and peers can provide invaluable support and guidance. A dedicated support network offers different perspectives, shares knowledge, and provides encouragement. Building and maintaining a robust network can help you navigate challenges and stay motivated.

Executing the Plan

Executing your strategic plan requires focused action and adaptability. Prioritizing high-impact activities and adjusting strategies as needed are critical to successful execution.

Focused Action

Prioritizing high-impact activities ensures that your efforts are directed toward the most significant tasks. This involves setting clear priorities and focusing on actions that will yield the highest returns. Focused action helps you make the most of your time and resources.

Adaptability

It is crucial to be ready to adjust your strategies in response to changing circumstances. Adaptability allows you to pivot when necessary and take advantage of new opportunities. It ensures that your plan remains relevant and effective over time.

Chapter 3: Building Momentum and Gaining a Burst of Energy

Sources of Motivation

Motivation is the driving force behind persistence and achievement. Understanding and harnessing various sources of motivation can help you build and sustain momentum.

Intrinsic Motivation

Intrinsic motivation comes from within and is driven by personal satisfaction and a sense of accomplishment. Finding internal drivers for  persistence, such as passion, curiosity, and a desire for self-improvement, can provide a robust and sustainable source of motivation.

Extrinsic Motivation

Extrinsic motivation involves external rewards, such as recognition, financial incentives, and career advancement. Boosting efforts with external rewards can be effective, especially when combined with intrinsic motivation. This dual approach ensures that you remain motivated throughout your journey.

Techniques for Building Momentum

Building momentum involves achieving early successes and making steady progress. These techniques can help you gain and maintain momentum.

Quick Wins

Achieving early successes, or "quick wins," can build confidence and create a positive feedback loop. Quick wins provide immediate rewards and boost morale, encouraging you to continue pushing forward.

Incremental Progress

Making steady, consistent advancements is critical to building momentum. Breaking tasks into smaller steps and celebrating each milestone keeps you motivated and maintains forward momentum. Incremental progress ensures that you are continuously moving towards your larger goals.

Maintaining High Energy Levels

High energy levels are essential for sustaining effort and maintaining focus. This involves taking care of both your physical and mental well-being.

Physical Well-Being

Physical well-being is the foundation of high energy levels. Regular exercise, a balanced diet, and sufficient rest are crucial for maintaining physical health and stamina. Prioritizing your physical well-being ensures you have the energy to tackle challenges and stay persistent.

Mental Well-Being

Mental well-being is equally important. Techniques for managing stress, such as mindfulness, meditation, and relaxation exercises, can help you stay focused and resilient. Maintaining a positive mindset and taking time for mental relaxation is essential for sustaining high energy levels and staying motivated.

Chapter 4: Innovation and Creativity in Outperforming Competitors

Role of Innovation

Innovation is a crucial driver of competitive advantage. It involves creating novel solutions, improving processes, and differentiating yourself from competitors.

Creating Competitive Advantage

Using innovation to stand out involves developing unique solutions and approaches that  set you apart. This can include introducing new products or services, improving existing ones, or finding more efficient ways to deliver value. Innovation helps you maintain a competitive edge and stay ahead of rivals.

Solving Problems

Innovative solutions to familiar challenges can provide significant advantages. This involves thinking creatively and approaching problems from new angles. Solving problems through innovation enhances your performance and positions you as a leader in your field.

Encouraging Creativity

Encouraging Creativity is essential for fostering innovation. Brainstorming, mind mapping, and collaborative thinking can help generate the latest ideas and approaches.

Creative Thinking Techniques

Brainstorming sessions, mind mapping, and other creative thinking techniques can help you generate many ideas. These methods encourage free thinking and exploration, leading to innovative solutions and breakthroughs.

Collaborative Innovation

Working with others to generate current ideas can enhance Creativity and innovation. Collaborative innovation involves combining diverse perspectives and skills to develop and refine ideas. This approach leverages a team's strengths and fosters a culture of Creativity and continuous improvement.

Implementing Innovations

Turning innovative ideas into reality requires testing, iteration, and scaling. This involves developing and refining ideas and expanding their impact once they prove successful.

Testing and Iteration

Developing and refining innovative ideas through testing and iteration is crucial for success. This involves experimenting with different approaches, gathering feedback, and making necessary adjustments. Testing and iteration ensure that your innovations are effective and practical.

Scaling Successful Innovations

Once an innovation proves successful, expanding its impact is the next step. Scaling involves increasing the scope and reach of the innovation, ensuring that it delivers maximum value. This can include replicating the innovation across different areas or markets or enhancing its features to meet broader needs.

Chapter 5: Leveraging Your Unique Strengths and Blowing Past the Competition

Identifying Strengths

Understanding and leveraging your unique strengths is critical to outperforming competitors. This involves self-assessment and feedback from others to comprehensively understand your abilities.

Self-Assessment

Self-assessment is the process of evaluating your skills and talents. This involves reflecting  on your experiences, identifying your strengths, and recognizing areas for improvement. Self-assessment helps you understand what you excel at and how to leverage these strengths to achieve your goals.

Feedback from Others

Gaining insights from colleagues, mentors, and peers can provide valuable perspectives on your strengths. Feedback from others can highlight strengths you may not have recognized and offer guidance on developing them further. Constructive feedback is essential for continuous improvement and maximizing your capabilities.

Maximizing Strengths

Once you have identified your strengths, maximizing them involves continuous development and strategic application. This ensures that your strengths contribute effectively to your success.

Skill Development

Continually improving your key strengths is essential for staying competitive. This involves seeking out opportunities for learning and growth, such as training programs, workshops, and practical experience. Skill development ensures that your strengths remain relevant and impactful.

Using Strengths Strategically

Applying your strengths to achieve goals involves strategic planning and execution. This means identifying situations where your strengths can significantly impact you and aligning your efforts accordingly. Strategically using strengths enhances your effectiveness and efficiency.

Amplifying Capabilities through Collaboration

Collaboration can amplify your strengths and enhance your overall capabilities. This involves building effective teams and leveraging connections to support your efforts.

Team Dynamics

Building effective teams that complement your strengths can enhance your performance. This involves selecting team members with diverse skills and perspectives, fostering a collaborative environment, and ensuring clear communication. Effective team dynamics lead to more incredible innovation and success.

Networking

Leveraging connections to enhance your capabilities involves building and maintaining a solid network. This includes engaging with mentors, industry experts, and peers who can offer support, advice, and opportunities. Networking provides access to resources and knowledge that amplify your strengths and contribute to your success.

Chapter 6: Overcoming Obstacles, Blowing Past the Competition, and Adapting to Change

Overcoming obstacles is a critical aspect and tests your resolve and adaptability. Internal barriers such as self-doubt and fear of failure are often challenging to overcome. These barriers can  hinder your progress and undermine your confidence. Building self-awareness is the first step in tackling these internal obstacles. By understanding your fears and doubts, you can develop strategies to address them. For instance, self-doubt can be mitigated through positive affirmations, seeking feedback, and celebrating small wins. On the other hand, fear of failure can be tackled by re-framing failure as a learning opportunity rather than a setback.

External challenges, such as industry changes and competition, require a strategic approach. Staying informed about trends and developments in your field can help you anticipate changes and prepare accordingly. This proactive approach ensures that you are not caught off guard by sudden shifts in the market. Developing contingency plans for various scenarios can provide a roadmap for navigating uncertainties. For instance, having a financial buffer can help you weather economic downturns while maintaining a diverse skill set can make you adaptable to changing job requirements.

Problem-solving techniques are essential tools for overcoming obstacles. Approaching challenges with a solution-focused mindset involves breaking down problems into manageable parts and identifying actionable steps. Root cause analysis, brainstorming, and mind mapping can help you understand the underlying issues and generate potential solutions. This systematic approach makes problems more manageable but reduces their stress and anxiety.

Resilience is another crucial trait for overcoming obstacles. Developing resilience involves building mental toughness and the ability to bounce back from setbacks. This can be achieved through mindfulness, meditation, and stress management techniques. Additionally, fostering a growth mindset can help you view challenges as opportunities for growth rather than insurmountable barriers. Embracing change and uncertainty with a positive attitude can significantly enhance your resilience.

Adapting to change is an integral part of maintaining persistence. Flexibility is crucial to staying in this ad. This means I am in a rapidly evolving world, open to current ideas, willing to take risks, and ready to pivot when necessary. Embracing change involves continuous learning and development. Keeping up with industry trends, acquiring new skills, and staying curious can help you remain relevant and competitive. Additionally, seeking feedback and being receptive to constructive criticism can provide valuable insights and guide your growth.

Connecting with a supportive network can help you navigate obstacles and adapt to change. Engaging with mentors, colleagues, and peers can provide different perspectives, share knowledge, and offer encouragement. Building a solid support network ensures you can access resources and guidance when facing challenges. Collaboration and teamwork can also enhance problem-solving capabilities and make overcoming obstacles more manageable.

Overcoming obstacles and adapting to change also requires a balance of steadfastness and flexibility. While staying committed to your goals is essential, it is equally crucial to be adaptable in your approach. This dynamic balance lets you focus on your objectives while remaining responsive to changing circumstances. It involves setting clear priorities and being willing to adjust your plans as needed. This flexibility ensures you can navigate obstacles effectively without losing sight of your long-term goals.

Celebrating your successes, no matter how small, can also boost your motivation and persistence. Recognizing and appreciating your achievements reinforces positive behavior and encourages continued effort. Celebrations can take various forms, from acknowledging milestones to rewarding yourself with small treats. This practice helps maintain a positive mindset and provides the motivation to keep pushing forward.

Reflecting on past challenges and how you overcame them can provide valuable insights and lessons for future obstacles. This reflection helps you understand your strengths and areas for improvement. It also reinforces your resilience and problem-solving skills. Keeping a journal or recording your experiences can help you reflect on your journey. It allows you to track progress, celebrate achievements, and learn from setbacks.

Maintaining a healthy work-life balance is essential for sustaining persistence and overcoming obstacles. Ensuring you have time for relaxation, hobbies, and social activities can prevent burnout and energize you. This balance also allows you to approach challenges with a fresh perspective and renewed vigor. Prioritizing self-care and well-being ensures you have the physical and mental stamina to persist through difficulties.

Understanding that setbacks are a natural part of the journey to success can help you maintain a positive attitude. Viewing obstacles as opportunities for growth rather than failures can change your perspective and enhance your resilience. This mindset shift allows you to embrace challenges with confidence and persistence. It also encourages you to take risks and explore new possibilities, knowing that setback-opening processes.

A long-term vision for your goals can provide a sense of purpose and direction. This vision acts as a guiding star, keeping you focused and motivated even in the face of an unexpected picture of what you want to achieve and why it matters. It can also inspire you to keep pushing forward. It also helps you make decisions that align with your long-term objectives, ensuring that your efforts are directed toward meaningful outcomes.

Leveraging your strengths and building on your successes can create a positive momentum that helps you overcome obstacles. Focusing on what you do well and continuously improving those skills can enhance your confidence and effectiveness. This approach ensures you always play to your strengths and maximize your potential. Additionally, seeking opportunities to apply your strengths in new and challenging situations can help you grow and develop further.

Finally, maintaining a sense of humor and a positive attitude can make overcoming obstacles more enjoyable and less stressful. Finding humor in challenging situations can lighten the mood and provide a fresh perspective. A positive attitude helps you stay optimistic and motivated, even when faced with difficulties. This approach ensures you can navigate obstacles with resilience and grace, turning challenges into opportunities for growth and success.

Chapter 7: Maintaining Your Lead, Blowing Past the Competition, and Sustaining Success

Maintaining your lead and sustaining success requires a combination of consistent performance, continuous improvement, and strategic planning. Consistent performance involves maintaining lofty standards and delivering reliable results over time. This  consistency builds trust and credibility, ensuring you remain a leader in your field. It consists in setting clear expectations, monitoring progress, and holding yourself accountable. Consistent performance is not just about working hard but also about working smart, focusing on high-impact activities, and prioritizing tasks that contribute to your long-term goals.

Continuous improvement is a mindset that drives you to constantly seek ways to enhance your performance and achieve better results. This involves regularly assessing your skills, seeking feedback, and identifying areas for growth. Embracing a culture of continuous improvement ensures that you remain competitive and adaptable. It encourages you to stay curious, explore innovative ideas, and experiment with different approaches. This proactive approach helps you stay ahead of the competition and sustain your success over time.

Managing success is another critical aspect of maintaining your lead. Success can sometimes lead to complacency, where you become satisfied with your achievements and stop striving for further improvement. Avoiding complacency involves staying motivated and continuously setting higher objectives. This means celebrating your successes and recognizing that there is always room for growth. It involves taking on new challenges and pushing yourself to achieve greater heights.

Setting new goals is essential for sustaining success. Once you achieve a goal, you must set new targets that challenge and keep you engaged. These goals should be aligned with your long-term vision and provide a sense of purpose and direction. Setting new goals ensures we are always moving forward and striving for excellence. It keeps you motivated and focused on achieving your highest potential.

Sustainable practices are crucial for long-term success. Developing habits that support ensures that you can earn your earnings over time. This includes regular exercise, healthy eating, and adequate rest. It also involves managing stress and maintaining a healthy work-life balance. Sustainable practices ensure you have the energy and resilience to persist through challenges and maintain high performance levels.

Legacy building is an essential aspect of sustaining success. Creating a lasting impact and preparing for future challenges involves thinking beyond your immediate goals. It means considering how your actions and achievements can benefit others and contribute to a larger purpose. Building a legacy involves engaging others, sharing your knowledge, and supporting initiatives aligning with your values. It ensures that your success has a positive and lasting impact on your community and industry.

Staying ahead requires a proactive approach to continuous improvement and innovation. This means regularly assessing your performance, seeking new opportunities, and staying informed about industry trends. It involves being open to change and willing to take risks. Staying ahead also involves building a solid support network and leveraging connections to enhance your capabilities. This proactive approach ensures that you remain a leader in your field and continue to achieve outstanding results.

Developing strategic partnerships can enhance your capabilities and support sustained success. Collaborating with others who share your vision and values can provide valuable resources and insights. Strategic alliances can help you expand your reach, access new markets, and enhance innovation efforts. Building and maintaining solid partnerships ensures you have the support and resources to sustain your success.

Regularly reviewing and reflecting on your achievements can provide valuable insights and guide your future. This involves taking time to assess progress, celebrate, and learn from your success on your journey and helps you understand what worked well and what could be improved. It provides a foundation for setting new goals and developing strategies for continuous improvement.

Embracing a growth mindset is essential for maintaining your lead and sustaining success. A growth mindset involves viewing challenges as opportunities for growth and believing that your abilities can be developed through effort and learning. This mindset encourages you to embrace challenges, persist through difficulties, and continuously seek improvement. It ensures that you remain adaptable and resilient, ready to overcome any obstacles that come your way.

Investing in your personal and professional development is crucial for sustaining success. This involves seeking opportunities for learning and growth, such as training programs, workshops, and mentorship. Investing in your development ensures you stay updated with industry trends and continue enhancing your skills. It also demonstrates a commitment to continuous improvement and a desire to achieve your highest potential.

Maintaining a positive and supportive work environment can enhance your performance and sustain your success. This involves fostering a culture of collaboration, respect, and mutual support. A positive work environment encourages Creativity, innovation, and high performance. It also provides a sense of belonging and motivation, ensuring you remain engaged and committed to your goals.

Effective time management is essential for maintaining your lead and sustaining success. This involves prioritizing tasks, setting clear goals, and managing time efficiently. Effective time management ensures that you focus on high-impact activities and avoid distractions. It also helps you maintain a healthy work-life balance and prevents burnout.

Developing resilience is crucial to sustaining critical success. This involves building mental toughness and the ability to bounce back from setbacks. Resilience ensures that you can navigate challenges and maintain your performance over time. It requires mindfulness, stress management, and maintaining a positive mindset. Building resilience ensures that you can sustain success and continue to achieve results.

Finally, maintaining a sense of purpose and passion for your work is essential for success. This involves being true to your values and what drives you. A sense of purpose motivates and inspires you to remain committed to your goals. It enhances your resilience and perseverance, helps you overcome obstacles, and maintains your lead.

Chapter 8: The Psychological Benefits of Persistence and Blowing Past the Competition

Persistence offers numerous psychological benefits that enhance your overall well-being and performance. One of the key benefits is the development of self-confidence. As you persist through challenges and achieve your goals, you  build a keen sense of self-efficacy. This confidence in your abilities encourages you to take on new challenges and strive for higher achievements. The process of overcoming obstacles and achieving success reinforces your belief in yourself and your capabilities.

Another significant psychological benefit of persistence is reduced anxiety. Having a clear, persistent focus provides a sense of control and direction. This clarity reduces the uncertainty and ambiguity that often cause anxiety. Knowing that you are taking consistent steps toward your goals provides reassurance and peace of mind. It helps you manage stress and stay calm even in challenging situations.

Persistence also enhances your problem-solving skills. The process of persisting through challenges requires you to think critically and creatively. It involves analyzing problems, exploring different solutions, and making informed decisions. This continuous practice sharpens your analytical and problem-solving abilities. Over time, you become more adept at finding practical solutions and navigating complex situations.

Improved focus and concentration are additional cognitive benefits of persistence. The discipline required to stay persistent enhances your ability to concentrate on tasks. It trains your mind to stay focused and avoid distractions. This improved focus enhances your productivity and efficiency. It ensures you can dedicate your full attention to high-priority tasks and achieve better results.

Emotional resilience is another critical aspect of persistence. Persisting through challenges builds one's capacity to handle stress and adversity. It teaches one to stay positive and composed in tricky situations. Emotional resilience ensures one can bounce back from setbacks and maintain performance. It enhances one's ability to cope with challenges and continue moving forward.

Maintaining a persistent attitude also fosters a sense of purpose and fulfillment. Working towards meaningful goals provides a sense of direction and motivation. It gives you a reason to persevere and strive for excellence. The feeling of accomplishment that comes from achieving your goals enhances your overall satisfaction and happiness. It reinforces the importance of persistence and encourages you to keep pushing forward.

Persistence also promotes a growth mindset. This mindset involves believing that your abilities can be developed through effort and learning. A growth mindset encourages you to embrace challenges and view failures as opportunities for growth. It fosters a positive attitude towards learning and development. This mindset shift enhances your resilience and persistence, ensuring you can achieve your highest potential.

Emotional intelligence is the process of persisting through challenging situations. It involves understanding and managing one's emotions, as well as recognizing and empathizing with the feelings of others. Emotional intelligence enhances interpersonal skills and relationships, ensuring one can navigate social situations effectively and build strong connections. This skill is essential for leadership and teamwork.

Building a persistent attitude also enhances your self-discipline and self-control. Staying committed to your goals requires managing your impulses and staying focused on your long-term objectives. This discipline ensures that you can resist distractions and maintain your efforts. Self-discipline enhances your ability to prioritize tasks and manage your time effectively. It ensures that you can achieve your goals and maintain high-performance levels.

Another psychological benefit of persistence is increased motivation and drive. Persistence is the process of setting and achieving motivation. Each success reinforces your desire to keep pushing forward. This positive feedback loop enhances your motivation and commitment. It ensures that you remain engaged and dedicated to your goals.

Persistence also fosters a sense of autonomy and control over your life. Taking consistent action in one's life. Consistent action toward one's empowerment. It reinforces the belief that you can shape your future and achieve good outcomes. This sense of control enhances your overall well-being and satisfaction. It ensures that you can navigate challenges with confidence and determination.

The psychological benefits of persistence extend to improved mental health and well-being. Staying focused on your goals and making consistent progress can reduce symptoms of depression and anxiety. It provides a sense of purpose and fulfillment, enhancing your overall happiness. The positive impact of persistence on mental health reinforces its importance for personal and professional success.

Persistence also enhances your ability to manage and regulate your emotions. Overcoming obstacles and achieving goals requires you to stay composed and focused. This emotional regulation ensures that you can handle stress and adversity effectively. It enhances your resilience and persistence, ensuring you can maintain your performance and achieve your goals.

Finally, the psychological benefits of persistence include enhanced creativity and innovation. Persisting through challenges encourages you to think freely and explore innovative solutions. This creative thinking enhances your problem-solving abilities and innovation efforts. It ensures you can find practical solutions and stay ahead of the competition.

Chapter 9: Inspiring Others, Blow Past the Competition, and Leading by Example

Inspiring others and leading by example is a powerful way to amplify your impact and achieve your goals. Leadership qualities such as vision, integrity, and trust are essential for inspiring others. An unclouded vision provides direction and motivation. It articulates a compelling future that others can strive towards. This vision inspires others to align their efforts and work towards common goals.

Integrity and trust are foundational qualities of effective leadership. Leading by example involves demonstrating consistent, ethical behavior. These build trust and credibility, ensuring that others follow your lead. Integrity is staying true to our values and principles, even in challenging situations. It ensures that your actions align with your words and builds a solid foundation of trust.

Mentorship is a powerful way to inspire and support others. Providing guidance and sharing knowledge can help others achieve their goals and overcome challenges. Mentorship involves offering support, feedback, and encouragement. It fosters a culture of collaboration and continuous improvement. Mentoring others enhances your leadership skills and ensures that knowledge and experience are passed on.

Supporting peers and colleagues is another way to inspire and lead by example. Helping, sharing resources, encouraging teamwork, and fostering collaboration fosters a positive work environment and improves overall performance. It ensures that everyone feels valued and motivated to contribute their best efforts.

Sharing your knowledge and experiences can provide valuable insights and inspiration to others. This involves being open and transparent about your journey, including your successes and setbacks. Sharing your story can inspire others to persist through challenges and strive for their goals. It provides practical lessons and reinforces the importance of perseverance and resilience.

Creating a positive impact involves engaging in activities that support your community and promote your values. This can include volunteering, supporting charitable causes, and advocating for social issues. Engaging in community activities enhances your leadership impact and demonstrates your commitment to making a difference. It inspires others to get involved and contribute to positive change.

Advocacy involves promoting causes and initiatives that align with your values and vision. This can include raising awareness, supporting policies, and mobilizing resources. Advocacy amplifies your impact and inspires others to act. It demonstrates your commitment to your values and encourages others to join your efforts.

Creating a positive work environment is essential for inspiring and leading by example. This involves fostering a culture of respect, collaboration, and mutual support. A positive work environment enhances motivation, Creativity, and performance. It ensures that everyone feels valued and motivated to contribute their best efforts.

Recognizing and celebrating the achievements of others is a powerful way to inspire and motivate. Acknowledging the efforts and  successes of your team members builds morale and encourages continued effort. Celebrations can take various forms, from public recognition to small rewards. This practice reinforces positive behavior and fosters a culture of appreciation and motivation.

Leading by example involves demonstrating resilience and perseverance. Navigating challenges and persevering through difficulties inspires others to do the same. It provides a practical model for overcoming obstacles and achieving goals. Demonstrating resilience reinforces the importance of persistence and encourages others to stay committed to their goals.

Effective communication is another critical aspect of inspiring and leading by example. Clear and transparent communication ensures everyone understands the vision, goals, and expectations. It fosters a culture of openness and trust. Effective communication involves active listening, providing feedback, and ensuring one feels heard and valued.

Encouraging Creativity and innovation is essential for inspiring others. This involves  creating an environment where innovative ideas are welcomed and explored. Encouraging Creativity fosters a culture of continuous improvement and innovation. It ensures that everyone feels empowered to contribute their ideas and solutions.

Building a diverse and inclusive team can enhance your leadership impact and inspire others. Diversity brings different perspectives and ideas, fostering Creativity and innovation. Inclusivity ensures that everyone feels valued and respected. Building a diverse and inclusive team enhances overall performance and creates a positive work environment.

Staying connected with your team and providing ongoing support is essential for effective leadership. Regular check-ins, feedback sessions, and team-building activities ensure everyone feels supported and motivated. Ongoing support enhances teamwork and collaboration, ensuring everyone is aligned and working towards common goals.

Finally, leading by example involves maintaining humility and confidence involves valuing the contributions of others and being open to feedback. Confidence consists of believing in your abilities and staying committed to your vision. Balancing humility and confidence ensures you can inspire and lead effectively, creating a positive and motivating environment.

Chapter 10: Reflecting on Your Journey, Blow Past the Competition, and Future Planning

Reflecting on your journey is a crucial aspect of personal and professional growth. Reviewing your achievements allows you to recognize and celebrate your successes. This celebration  reinforces positive behavior and motivates you to keep pushing forward. It provides a sense of accomplishment and boosts your confidence. Recognizing your achievements also helps you understand what strategies worked well and how you can replicate them in the future.

Learning from your experiences involves reflecting on both your successes and setbacks. Analyzing your setbacks provides valuable insights into areas for improvement. It helps you understand the reasons behind your challenges and develop strategies to overcome them. Reflecting on your experiences ensures that you learn from your mistakes and continue to grow and improve.

Setting future goals is essential for maintaining momentum and achieving continuous growth. Once you have reviewed your achievements and learned from your experiences,  the next step is to establish targets. These goals should be aligned with your long-term vision and provide a sense of purpose and direction. Setting future goals ensures that you remain motivated and focused on achieving your highest potential.

Lifelong learning is a crucial aspect of future planning. Committing to continuous growth and development ensures you stay updated with industry trends and enhance your skills. This proactive approach helps you remain competitive and adaptable. Lifelong learning involves seeking opportunities for training, education, and personal development. It ensures that you continue to evolve and achieve your goals.

Leaving a legacy involves thinking beyond your immediate goals and considering how your actions can benefit others. Creating a lasting impact involves consisting of others, sharing your knowledge, and supporting initiatives that align with your values. Building a legacy ensures that your success has a positive and lasting impact on your community and industry. It provides a sense of fulfillment and reinforces the importance of persistence and leadership.

Reflecting on your journey also involves considering the impact of your actions on others. This includes understanding how your achievements have inspired and supported those around you. Recognizing your positive influence on others reinforces the importance of leading by example. It encourages you to continue inspiring and helping others as you pursue your goals.

Future planning involves setting an unclouded vision for what you want to achieve. This vision acts as a guiding star, providing direction and motivation. It helps you stay focused on your long-term objectives and make decisions that  align with your goals. An unobstructed vision ensures that your efforts are directed toward meaningful outcomes and enhances your sense of purpose.

Establishing new challenges and pushing yourself to achieve greater heights is essential for continuous growth. Setting ambitious goals ensures that you remain engaged and motivated. It encourages you to step out of your comfort zone and explore new possibilities. Taking on new challenges enhances your resilience and persistence, ensuring you continue growing and achieving outstanding results.

Building and maintaining a solid support network is crucial for future planning. Engaging with mentors, colleagues, and peers provides valuable insights, guidance, and encouragement. A fanatical support network ensures you have access to resources and support as you pursue your goals. It enhances your resilience and persistence, ensuring you navigate challenges and achieve your objectives.

Regularly reviewing and adjusting your plans ensures that you stay on track and remain adaptable. This involves assessing your progress, celebrating your successes, and making necessary adjustments to your strategies. Regular review and adjustment ensure that your plans remain relevant and practical. Practically, you stay focused on your goals and maintain momentum.

Future planning also involves considering the skills and knowledge you will need to achieve your goals. This consists of identifying growth areas and seeking opportunities for learning and development. Developing a clear plan for skill enhancement ensures that you stay competitive and prepared for future challenges. It enhances your confidence and ability to achieve your goals.

Maintaining a positive and resilient mindset is essential for future planning. This involves staying optimistic and motivated, even in the face of challenges. A positive mindset ensures that you can navigate obstacles with confidence and persistence. It enhances your resilience and ability to achieve long-term success.

Regular reflection and meditation can provide valuable insights and clarity for future planning. Reflecting on your journey and considering your goals ensures you stay connected to your values and vision. Reflection and meditation enhance your self-awareness and provide a sense of calm and focus.

Finally, future planning involves celebrating your journey and recognizing your progress. Acknowledging your achievements and the lessons you have learned reinforces the importance of persistence and resilience. It provides motivation and inspiration for continuing to pursue your goals. Celebrating your journey ensures that you remain focused on your long-term vision and strive for excellence.

Persistence Conclusion

Persistence is the key to achieving long-term success and blowing past the competition. This guide has explored various strategies for setting  clear and achievable goals, developing strategic plans, building momentum, and leveraging your unique strengths. Each chapter has provided practical insights and techniques for maintaining persistence, overcoming obstacles, and inspiring others. By embracing these principles and committing to continuous growth and development, you can achieve your highest potential and leave a legacy. Remember, the journey to success is a marathon, not a sprint. Stay persistent, stay focused, and keep pushing forward. Your goals are within reach, and your potential is limitless.

Final Thought: Embrace Persistence, Blow Past the Competition and Achieve Your Dreams

Revisiting the Theme of Persistence

Persistence is more than a trait; it is a lifestyle choice that permeates every aspect of our lives. Throughout this book, we have delved into the essential strategies and mindsets that can help you surpass the competition and reach your goals. Persistence has been the common thread, from setting SMART goals and developing strategic plans to leveraging your unique strengths and building momentum. The power of persistence lies in its ability to transform obstacles into opportunities, failures into learning experiences, and dreams into reality.

The Paradox of Persistence

Persistence is both a gift and a challenge. It empowers you to keep pushing forward but demands resilience and sacrifice. Understanding this paradox is crucial. While persistence can  lead to burnout if not appropriately managed, it also builds the mental and emotional fortitude necessary to succeed. Embracing this duality means recognizing when to push through and when to rest, ensuring that your journey is sustainable and fulfilling.

The Power of Momentum

A burst of momentum can be the difference between stagnation and success. Achieving quick wins, celebrating small victories, and maintaining high energy levels are vital for sustaining momentum. This dynamic energy propels you forward, making overcoming challenges easier and staying focused on your goals. Momentum is not just about speed but about maintaining consistent progress and building on each success to reach new heights.

Straightforward Solutions

Persistence does not have to be complicated. Often, the most straightforward solutions are the most effective. Whether breaking goals down into manageable tasks, seeking feedback, or maintaining a positive mindset, straightforward strategies can have a profound impact. These practical approaches make persistence accessible and achievable, ensuring that anyone can harness its power to succeed.

Inspirational Stories

History is replete with stories of individuals who have succeeded through persistence. Consider Thomas Edison, who famously failed thousands of times before inventing the light bulb. Or J.K. Rowling, whose persistence turned her into one of the most successful authors despite numerous rejections.

These stories remind us that persistence is often the most significant factor in achieving greatness. They inspire us to keep pushing forward, even when the path seems impossible.

The Role of Community

No one succeeds alone. Building a supportive network of mentors, peers, and colleagues is crucial for sustaining persistence. These relationships provide encouragement, feedback, and growth opportunities. Engaging with a community of like-minded individuals can amplify your efforts and keep you motivated. Collaboration and support are the bedrock of persistent success.

The Impact of Innovation

Innovation is a critical component of blowing past the competition. It involves continually  seeking new and better ways to achieve your goals. Embracing Creativity and being willing to take risks can set you apart and provide a competitive edge. Innovation requires persistence to experiment, iterate, and refine ideas until they become successful solutions.

Lifelong Learning

Persistence is linked to a commitment to lifelong learning. The world is constantly changing, and staying ahead requires a willingness to adapt and grow. This means seeking new knowledge, skills, and experiences that enhance your abilities and broaden your horizons. Lifelong learning ensures that you remain relevant and capable of achieving your goals in a dynamic environment.

Building a Legacy

Creating a legacy involves thinking beyond your immediate goals and considering the broader impact of your actions. Persistence in building a legacy means consistently working towards making a positive difference in your community and industry. It involves mentoring others, sharing your knowledge, and supporting initiatives that align with your values. A legacy is not built overnight; it is the culmination of persistent effort and dedication.

Reflecting on Your Journey

Regular reflection is essential for sustaining persistence. Reviewing your progress, celebrating your achievements, and learning from setbacks provide valuable insights and reinforce your commitment. Reflection helps you stay connected to your goals and ensures that you are continuously improving and adapting. It is a powerful tool for maintaining motivation and focus.

Setting Future Goals

Once you have achieved your current goals, setting new, ambitious targets is essential for  maintaining momentum. Future goals should challenge you and provide a sense of purpose and direction. They ensure that you remain engaged and motivated, continuously striving for excellence. Setting future goals is a testament to your persistent spirit and desire for growth.

Balancing Ambition and Well-Being

Persistence requires a delicate balance between ambition and well-being. While striving for success is essential, taking care of your physical and mental health is equally crucial. Maintaining a healthy work-life balance, practicing self-care, and seeking support ensure that your persistence is sustainable. This balance prevents burnout and enhances your overall quality of life.

The Importance of Resilience

Resilience is the backbone of persistence. It is the ability to bounce back from setbacks and keep moving forward. Building resilience involves developing coping strategies, maintaining a positive mindset, and staying flexible in the face of change. Resilience ensures that you can weather any storm and continue to pursue your goals with determination and strength.

Celebrating Small Wins

Celebrating small wins is a powerful way to sustain persistence. Each achievement reinforces each achievement of our progress and boosts our motivation. Acknowledging and appreciating these victories creates a positive feedback loop that encourages continued effort. It reminds you that every step forward, however small, brings you closer to your goal.

Embracing Change

Change is inevitable, and embracing it is crucial for persistence. Staying adaptable and open to new possibilities ensures you can navigate uncertainties and seize opportunities.  Embracing change involves a willingness to pivot, experiment, and explore new directions. This flexibility enhances your ability to persist through challenges and achieve long-term success.

Final Thoughts

Persistence is not just a strategy; it is a way of life. It is the unwavering commitment to your goals, the resilience to overcome obstacles, and the passion to keep pushing forward. By embracing persistence, you unlock your potential and open the door to limitless possibilities. This book has provided the tools, strategies, and inspiration needed to harness the power of persistence and achieve your dreams. Remember, the journey to success is a marathon, not a sprint. Stay persistent, stay focused, and keep pushing forward. Your goals are within reach, and your potential is limitless.

Persistence is not just a strategy but a way of life. It is the unwavering commitment to your goals, the resilience to overcome obstacles, and the passion to keep pushing forward. By embracing persistence, you unlock your potential and open the door to limitless possibilities. This book has provided the tools, strategies, and inspiration needed to harness the power of persistence and achieve your dreams. Remember, the journey to success is a marathon, not a sprint. Stay persistent, stay focused, and keep pushing forward. Your goals are within reach, and your potential is limitless.

When discussing persistence as a way of life, we dive into a philosophy that permeates every aspect of our existence. It's not just about sticking to a plan or a schedule; it's about adopting a mindset that refuses to accept defeat, no matter the odds. Think of persistence as the steadfast ship navigating through the stormy seas of life. This ship doesn't just float aimlessly, hoping to arrive somewhere favorable. It has a destination, a purpose, and a captain who is resolute in steering through the turbulent waters, with eyes fixed firmly on the horizon.

The beauty of persistence lies in its transformative power. It is the force that takes ordinary individuals and molds them into extraordinary achievers. Every obstacle encountered is not a setback but a steppingstone, a crucial part of the journey that strengthens resolve and sharpens skills. Consider the story of Thomas Edison, who famously failed thousands of times before perfecting the electric light bulb. Each failure was a lesson, a necessary detour that provided invaluable insights and inched him closer to success. Edison's persistence was not merely a tactic but an intrinsic part of his being, an unshakeable belief that success was not just possible but inevitable.

Resilience is a critical component of persistence, acting as the armor that shields you from the slings and arrows of adversity. It's the ability to bounce back from failures, rejections, and disappointments, each time stronger and more determined. Imagine a rubber band being stretched to its limits. Every time it snaps back, it retains its original shape, ready to be stretched again. This elasticity is what resilience brings to the table in the grand persistence scheme. It's about maintaining your core purpose and passion, regardless of how often life attempts to pull you in different directions.

Passion is the fuel that powers the engine of persistence. Without passion, persistence would be a hollow, mechanical act. Passion provides the why behind the what, the compelling reason that drives you to keep going even when the going gets tough. It turns a job into a calling, a challenge into an opportunity, and a dream into a reality. Think of the most successful individuals across various fields—athletes, artists, entrepreneurs. What they all have in common is a deep-seated passion for what they do. This passion makes the sacrifices, the late nights, and the endless grind bearable and invigorating.

By embracing persistence, you open the door to limitless possibilities. This isn't just motivational rhetoric; it's a fundamental truth about human potential. When you commit to a goal with unwavering persistence, you see opportunities where others see obstacles. You find solutions where others find problems. Your mind becomes attuned to success, actively seeking ways to turn your vision into reality. It is like having a sixth sense that guides you through the maze of life, always pointing you toward your goal.

This book has provided the tools, strategies, and inspiration needed to harness the power of persistence. Tools like time management, goal setting, and self-discipline are the details that hold your persistence machinery together. Strategies such as breaking down big goals into manageable tasks, seeking continuous feedback, and adapting to changing circumstances are the gears that keep this machinery running smoothly. Inspiration comes from the stories of those who have walked the path before you, faced similar challenges, and emerged victorious. These elements combine to create a comprehensive guide that equips you to tackle any goal with confidence and tenacity.

Remember, the journey to success is a marathon, not a sprint. This metaphor underscores the importance of pacing yourself, maintaining steady progress, and conserving energy for the long haul. In a marathon, the runners who sprint at the start often find themselves exhausted halfway through, while those who maintain a consistent pace steadily advance toward the finish line. Similarly, in pursuing your goals, staying focused and persistent over the long term is crucial. There will be times when progress seems slow when the finish line is moving further away rather than closer. These moments test your resolve, challenge you to dig deep, and help you find the strength to keep moving forward.

Stay persistent, stay focused, and keep pushing forward. These words are more than just a mantra; they are a call to action, a reminder that persistence is not a passive state but an active pursuit. It requires constant effort and a deliberate choice to persevere despite difficulties. Focus is the lens through which persistence is directed. Without focus, your efforts can become scattered and ineffective. It is about keeping your eyes on the prize, continually reminding yourself of why you started and what you hope to achieve.

Your goals are within reach, and your potential is limitless. This statement encapsulates the essence of what it means to live a life of persistence. It is about believing in your ability to achieve great things, regardless of obstacles. It is about recognizing that your potential is not fixed but expandable, limited only by your willingness to push the boundaries. When you adopt this mindset, every challenge becomes an opportunity for growth, and every setback a chance to learn and improve.

Persistence, resilience, and passion form a trifecta that can propel you towards your dreams. They are the bedrock upon which outstanding achievements are built. By integrating these qualities into your daily life, you cultivate an unshakeable sense of purpose and direction. You become the captain of your ship, navigating through the storms with confidence and clarity, always moving towards your destination.

In conclusion, persistence is more than just a strategy; it is a way of life. It is the commitment to your goals, the resilience to overcome obstacles, and the passion to keep pushing forward. By embracing persistence, you unlock your potential and open the door to limitless possibilities. This book has provided the tools, strategies, and inspiration needed to harness the power of persistence and achieve your dreams. Remember, the journey to success is a marathon, not a sprint. Stay persistent, stay focused, and keep pushing forward. Your goals are within reach, and your potential is limitless. When adopted wholeheartedly, this philosophy has the power to transform your life, turning your dreams into reality and your aspirations into achievements.

Persistence is not just a strategy but a way of life. It is the unwavering commitment to your goals, the resilience to overcome obstacles, and the passion to keep pushing forward. By embracing persistence, you unlock your potential and open the door to limitless possibilities. This book has provided the tools, strategies, and inspiration needed to harness the power of persistence and achieve your dreams. Remember, the journey to success is a marathon, not a sprint. Stay persistent, stay focused, and keep pushing forward. Your goals are within reach, and your potential is limitless.

Persistence would be the "extra life" cheat code if life were a video game. It keeps you going even when you have hit all the spikes, fallen into lava pits and faced the ultimate boss of procrastination. Imagine Mario giving up because he could not find the suitable warp pipe—no more princess rescues! So, don your metaphorical overalls, grab your persistence power-up, and keep jumping those hurdles.

Think of persistence as your GPS: no matter how many wrong turns or "recalculating routes" you face, it will always find a way to get you back on track. Sure, you might take a scenic route through the Land of Setbacks, but at least you'll have a pleasant view and a story to tell when you finally reach your destination.

Remember the tortoise and the hare? Spoiler alert: the tortoise wins, not because he's got turbocharged legs but because he understands the value of slow and steady progress. Meanwhile, the hare is off napping under a tree, dreaming of easy victories. So next time someone calls you slow, smile, and tell them you are in tortoise mode—cruising steadily towards success.

Persistence is like that stubborn piece of broccoli that refuses to go unnoticed on your plate. It may not always be the most glamorous or exciting quality, but it is the one that is packed with the nutrients you need for long-term success. And much like eating your greens, embracing persistence might be an acquired taste, but it sure pays off overall.

Have you ever tried squeezing toothpaste back into the tube? It's about as impossible as achieving your dreams without persistence. Sure, you can have the shiniest toothpaste tube on the block, but you're just stuck with minty frustration if you don't. Apply the pressure; you're the squeeze that gets things moving, ensuring you don't just sit there with a half-empty tube of potential.

Persistence and resilience go together like peanut butter and jelly. Separately, they make understanders together table t together he tables combo. Re-together silence helps you bounce back when your sandwich falls jelly, while persistence ensures you make another sandwich, no matter how many times it splats. So spread thick layers of both and enjoy the tasty journey to your goals.

Passion, on the other hand, is the fiery salsa to your persistence taco. It's what adds that extra zest and kick to your journey. Without passion, persistence might get a little bland and dry. Mix them together, though, and you've got something satisfying and irresistibly motivating. Just Remember to Keep a glass of water handy for things to get spicy.

Consider your goals as a mountain, and persistence as your trusty hiking boots. Those boots will take you over rough terrain, through muddy patches, and up steep inclines. Sure, there might be blisters along the way, but every step brings you closer to the summit. Plus, think of the view from the top—worth every ounce of effort and every Band-Aid.

You know those infomercials that promise six-pack abdominal muscles in just six minutes a day? Newsflash: they are selling you short. Actual results require real persistence. Imagine if Captain Crunch traded his cereal for a crunch workout regime—he would still need more than a commercial break to get in shape. So put in the time, stay persistent, and soon enough, you will be crunching your way to victory.

Persistence is like having a built-in spell checker for your life goals. It catches your mistakes, underlines them, and prompts you to keep the rewrite you get. It might not be unpleasant to see all those red squiggly lines, but without them, you would never know where you need to improve. So, embrace the squiggles—they are your roadmap to success.

Ever played Whack-a-Mole? That is persistence concisely. When you think you have one obstacle down, another one pops up. But instead of getting frustrated, you keep whacking away, knowing that each mole you conquer is a step closer to winning the game. Persistence is about keeping that mallet swinging, no matter how many annoying moles try to throw you off.

In the grand game of Monopoly, persistence is your Get Out of Jail Free card. You might land on tough spots, face financial ruin, or end up in prison, but with persistence, you always have a way to bounce back. Just keep your eye on the prize and roll those dice—eventually, you'll pass. Go and collect your reward.

Persistence is like a bad case of hiccups that just won't quit. It keeps popping up, reminding you to keep going, even when you'd instead hold your breath and hope it goes away. But unlike hiccups, persistence is something you want to stay around—it's the nagging reminder that your goals are worth the effort, no matter how many times you need to gulp for air.

Imagine if famous inventors gave up at the first sign of failure. We'd sit in the dark, sending messages via carrier pigeon and cooking over open flames. Edison didn't stop after the first failed light bulb, and Bell didn't quit after the first crossed wire. Their persistence illuminated the world and connected us all. So, when you face your next challenge, think WWED—What Would Edison Do?

Persistence is the duct tape of life—it fixes anything. Do you have a dream that's falling apart? Wrap it in a few layers of persistence. Facing a leaky motivation? Persistence will seal it right up. It may not be pretty, but it's robust, reliable, and always does the job. So, stock up on your metaphorical duct tape and start patching those dreams.

Picture persistence as the ever-persistent salesperson who will not take no for an answer. He keeps knocking on the door of your dreams, armed with the latest and most excellent strategies for success. Sure, you might try to hide behind the curtains, but deep down, you know he has got something valuable to offer. So, open the door, listen to the pitch, and buy into the power of persistence.

If life is a circus, then persistence is your tightrope-walking act. It requires balance, focus, and the courage to keep moving forward, even when the net below looks too far away. One misstep might wobble you, but you will persistently regain your footing and continue crossing to the other side. And when you finally make it, you will bow to the applause of your achievements.

Persistence is like trying to herd cats— frustrating, impossible, but rewarding when you finally gall-move in the right direction. Each cat represents a challenge or setback; with enough patience and determination, you can guide them all toward it. Plus, who does not love the idea of a well-herded dream-cat parade?

Consider your goals as seeds planted in the garden of life. Persistence is the watering can that ensures they grow, despite the weeds of doubt and the droughts of discouragement. It is the daily act of nurturing your dreams, knowing that with enough care and time, they will blossom into the beautiful garden you have always envisioned.

Imagine a squirrel preparing for winter—gathering nuts with relentless focus and determination. That is persistence in action. Even when the going gets tough, the squirrel does not give up. It climbs higher, digs deeper, and keeps on collecting, knowing that each nut is a step towards survival. Be the squirrel. Gather your nuts of progress and stash them away for future success.

Persistence is the unsung hero of the superhero world. Sure, it does not wear a cape or have a catchy name, but it is the driving force behind every heroic feat. Think about it—Batman did not become Gotham's protector overnight. He faced countless villains and endured innumerable setbacks but never gave up. So, channel your inner Dark Knight and keep fighting for your dreams.

If you have ever watched a nature documentary, you will know that even the smallest creatures exhibit incredible persistence. Take the dung beetle, for example, rolling its prized ball of dung uphill with unwavering determination. It might seem like a Sisyphean task, but that beetle knows the value of its efforts. So next time you feel like you are pushing uphill, remember the dung beetle—if it can persist, so can you.

Persistence is like learning to ride a unicycle—awkward, wobbly, and filled with falls, but exhilarating once you get the hang of it. You will start off flailing, even bruised, but with each attempt, you will find your balance. And soon enough, you will be pedaling forward with confidence, leaving onlookers in awe of your one-wheeled determination.

Imagine you are building a sandcastle on the beach. Every wave that comes is a setback, eroding your hard work. But persistence is what drives you to rebuild, repeatedly, each castle standing a little stronger than before. Eventually, you will create a masterpiece that even the mightiest wave cannot wash away. And if not, at least you have had a sandy suitable time trying.

Persistence is your personal er, always rooting for you from the sidelines, even when you feel like admitting defeat. It is the voice that shouts, "You've got this!" during the darkest moments. So put on your imaginary pom-poms, perform a high kick, and remember that with persistence, your inner cheerleader is always there to lift you up.

Persistence is your morning coffee—it wakes you up, gets you moving, and keeps you going throughout the day. Without it, you would be groggy, sluggish, and unmotivated. So, brew a fresh pot of determination every morning, sip on your persistence, and watch as you tackle your goals with the same energy as a caffeine-fueled squirrel on a mission.

Persistence is not just a strategy but a way of life. It is the unwavering commitment to your goals, the resilience to overcome obstacles, and the passion to keep pushing forward. By embracing persistence, you unlock your potential and open the door to limitless possibilities. This book has provided the tools, strategies, and inspiration needed to harness the power of persistence and achieve your dreams. Remember, the journey to success is a marathon, not a sprint. Stay persistent, stay focused, and keep pushing forward. Your goals are within reach, and your potential is limitless.

Let us compare persistence to trying to peel a particularly stubborn orange. No matter how tough the peel or how much juice squirts in your eye, you keep at it because you know the sweet, citrusy reward is worth it. Each stubborn segment you conquer is a small victory, and by the end, you are not just enjoying the fruit of your labor— you have also gotten a bit of a workout. Peel away those obstacles with zest, and you will be basking in the sweetness of success.

Think of persistence as your trusty Swiss Army knife. It is a multi-tool that equips you to handle any situation life throws your way. From opening cans of opportunity to cutting through the red tape of bureaucracy, persistence is the all-in-one gadget that ensures you are never stuck without a solution. Sure, it might not have the flair of a high-tech gizmo, but its reliability is second to none.

Persistence is like training a puppy. At first, it is all accidents and chewed-up shoes, but with time, patience, and a lot of "good boy" treats, you end up with a loyal companion who can do tricks and bring you joy. So, when your goals feel like a rambunctious puppy, remember that with consistent effort and a few motivational treats, you will have them sitting, staying, and rolling over in no time.

Imagine your goals are a jigsaw puzzle with a thousand tiny pieces. Persistence is the meticulous process of fitting each piece together, even when you are convinced you have lost a crucial corner. It's the satisfaction of seeing the bigger picture take shape, one frustratingly elusive piece at a time. Sure, you might spend hours looking for that one piece that completes the sky, but the final picture is always worth the hunt.

Persistence is your personal trainer, pushing you to do one more rep when you're ready to give up. It doesn't let you slack off or skip leg day. Instead, it keeps you accountable, reminding you that every effort brings you one step closer to your goals. And just like with a real trainer, you might not always love the tough love, but you'll appreciate the results.

Imagine trying to open a stubborn jar of pickles. At first, it seems impossible—no matter how hard you twist, the lid just won't budge. But persistence is the towel you grab for extra grip, the hot water you run over the lid, and the final, satisfying pop when it finally gives way. Each attempt builds your strength and determination, until you're the master of opening even the most recalcitrant jars of opportunity.

Persistence is like a boomerang. You might throw it out there and watch it veer off course, but with the proper technique and a bit of practice, it always comes back to you. Every time you throw your efforts into the world, persistence ensures they return with valuable lessons and experiences, guiding you closer to your target.

Ever watched a nature documentary featuring salmon swimming upstream? That's persistence in its most determined form. These fish battle currents, leap over obstacles, and evade predators to reach their spawning grounds. So, when life's current seems to be against you, channel your inner salmon and keep swimming upstream. You might just find your own spawning ground of success.

Persistence is the turtle in a world full of hares. While everyone else is sprinting and getting distracted, you're steadily plodding along, knowing that slow and steady wins the race. It's about maintaining a pace that's sustainable, even when the finish line seems far away. And when you finally cross that line, you'll do so with the satisfaction of knowing you didn't burn out or give up.

Think of persistence as the act of defrosting a stubborn windshield on a cold winter morning. At first, you're scraping away with no progress, but gradually, as the ice melts and your view clears, you're rewarded with the ability to see the road ahead. Persistence is what allows you to keep scraping away at your goals until the path to success is crystal clear.

Persistence is like a trusty old pair of jeans. They might not be the flashiest or the newest, but they're reliable, comfortable, and fit you just right. They've been with you through thick and thin and are always there to support you, even when the latest fashion trends come and go. So, wear your persistence with pride, knowing it's the perfect fit for achieving your dreams.

Ever tried knitting a sweater? It's a slow, methodical process, stitch by stitch, row by row. Persistence is what keeps you knitting, even when you drop a stitch or must unravel a row. Eventually, you end up with a cozy creation that's a testament to your patience and determination. So, when your goals feel like a tangled ball of yarn, keep knitting away—you'll have your warm and fuzzy moment.

Persistence is the sturdy root system of a mighty oak tree. While others might be swayed by the winds of doubt and adversity, your deep roots of determination keep you grounded. Over time, you grow taller and stronger, standing as a testament to the power of persistence. And just like that oak tree, you'll be able to weather any storm that comes your way.

Imagine your goals are a piñata, and persistence is the blindfolded whack you take with a bat. You might miss a few times, but with enough swings, you'll eventually have enough swings and enjoy the sweet rewards inside. No matter how off-target, each swing brings you closer to that candy-filled moment of triumph.

Persistence is like playing chess. It's about planning your moves, anticipating obstacles, and staying patient even when the game drags on. Every setback is an opportunity to reassess your strategy and make a comeback. And just like in chess, some of the most minor, most persistent moves lead to checkmate.

Picture yourself as an artist chiseling away at a block of marble. Persistence is the hammer and chisel you wield, slowly revealing the masterpiece hidden within. Every strike, no matter how small, shapes your vision into reality. It's a labor of love that requires patience, precision, and a lot of dust, but the final sculpture is worth every bit of effort.

Persistence is like learning to play an instrument. At first, it's all off-key notes and clumsy fingers, but with practice and determination, you start to create beautiful music. Each practice session, each missed note, is a step towards mastering your craft. So, keep playing, keep practicing, and soon you'll be hitting all the right notes on your journey to success.

Imagine your goals as a campfire and persistence as the fuel that keeps it burning. You must constantly add logs and stoke the flames, even when the fire seems to die. It's a continuous effort, but with persistence, you'll keep the fire of your dreams blazing brightly, providing warmth and light in the darkest of times.

Persistence is like a roller coaster ride. There are ups, downs, twists, and turns, but you hold on tight and keep moving forward. Even when the ride gets bumpy and you're tempted to close your eyes, persistence keeps you strapped in and ready for the next thrilling loop. And when you finally coast to a stop, you'll look back and realize it was the ride of a lifetime.

Think of persistence as the glue that holds together the puzzle pieces of your dreams. The sticky substance keeps everything in place, even when life tries to pull you apart. Without it, your goals would be a jumbled mess, but with persistence, you create a cohesive, beautiful picture that highlights your dedication and hard work.

Persistence is like learning to juggle. At first, you're dropping balls left and right, but with practice and patience, you start to find your rhythm. Each dropped ball is a lesson in coordination and focus. Eventually, you'll be effortlessly juggling your goals and impressing everyone around you with your persistence and skill.

Imagine your goals as a garden, and persistence as the act of weeding. It's not always glamorous or fun but ensuring your dreams can grow and thrive is necessary. Each weed you pull is an obstacle removed, a step closer to a flourishing, beautiful garden. So, grab your gloves, dig in, and keep weeding away the doubts and distractions.

Persistence is like baking a cake. You follow the recipe, measure the ingredients, and patiently wait for it to rise. Sometimes, things don't go as planned—the cake might sink or burn—but with each attempt, you learn and improve. And when you finally perfect the recipe, the sweet taste of success is more satisfying.

Think of persistence as a marathon training program. It's the daily runs, the sore muscles, and the commitment to keep going, even when you'd rather stay in bed. Each mile you log builds your endurance and brings you closer to the finish line. And when race day comes, you'll cross that line with the satisfaction of knowing your persistence paid off.

Persistence is like sculpting a sandcastle at the beach. The waves will try to wash it away, but you keep building, reinforcing, and perfecting your creation. Each tide is a challenge, but with determination, you can create a masterpiece that stands tall against the surf with determination. So, grab your bucket and spade, and start building your dreams, grain by grain.

Imagine persistence as a game of darts. Each throw is an attempt to hit the bull

eye of your goals. You might miss the mark several times, but with each throw, you adjust your aim and improve your technique. Persistence keeps you throwing, knowing you'll eventually hit that perfect score.

Persistence is like solving a Rubik's Cube. It's a puzzle that requires patience, strategy, and a lot of trial and error. Each twist and turn brings you closer to the solution, even when it feels like you're back at square one. Ke; soon and soon enough, you'll have all the colors aligned, a testament to your problem-solving prowess.

Think of persistence as learning to ride a bike. At first, it's all wobbles and falls, but with practice and determination, you find your balance and start pedaling with confidence. Each scraped knee is a reminder of your progress, and before you know it, you're cruising down the road to success, wind in your hair and a smile on your face.

Persistence is like planting a tree. It starts with a small sapling that requires consistent care —watering, pruning, and protecting it from pests. Over time, it grows into a strong, potent symbol of your hard work and dedication. So, plant your dreams, nurture them with persistence, and watch them grow into something magnificent.

Ladies and gentlemen welcome to this TED Talk on the powerhouse duo of persistence and determination. Now, I want you to imagine that you're about to embark on an adventure through life's wild, untamed jungle. You're going to need some trusty gear to make it through, and I'm here to tell you that persistence and determination are the ultimate survival tools. These aren't just your run-of-the-mill attributes—they are the Swiss Army knives of personal development.

Persistence is like your trusty compass in this jungle adventure. It points you towards your goals, keeping you on track even when the path is obscured by the thick foliage of doubt and distraction. Without it, you'd be wandering in circles, lost and frustrated. But with persistence, you have a clear direction and a way to navigate the maze of challenges that life throws your way.

Determination, on the other hand, is your machete. It's what you use to hack away at the obstacles blocking your path. Every swing cut through the vines of adversity, clearing a path towards your goals. It's hard work, and you might get a few scratches along the way, but determination ensures that nothing can stand in your way for long.

Persistence is the relentless drip of water that eventually wears down even the hardest stone. It's not about overwhelming force but about consistent, steady effort. Each drop might seem insignificant on its or time, it creates a path through the rock. So, be like water—persistent, patient, and unstoppable.

Imagine your goals as a high mountain peak. Persistence is your climbing rope, keeping you secure as you ascend. With each handhold and foothold, you inch closer to the summit. Sometimes, you feel like giving up when the air gets, and the climb becomes treacherous. But with persistence, you keep climbing, knowing that every step brings you closer to that breathtaking view from the top.

Determination is your crampons, the spikes that dig into the ice and give you traction on slippery slopes. They provide the grip you need to keep moving forward, even when the ground beneath you is unstable. Without determination, you'd be sliding backwards, losing precious ground. But with it, you can conquer even the most daunting peaks.

Persistence is like trying to untangle a ball of Christmas lights. At first, it seems like an impossible mess, a knotty nightmare that makes you want to throw the whole thing out. But with patience and persistence, you work through the tangles, unraveling each twist and turn until you have a perfectly functioning string of lights. And when you finally plug them in, the glow of your success is more satisfying.

Let's talk about the power of small steps. Persistence is the art of taking tiny, consistent steps towards your goals. It's like running a marathon, where each mile marker brings you closer to the finish line. Sure, it might feel slow at times, but remember, even a journey of a thousand miles begins with a single step. So, lace up those sneakers of determination and keep putting one foot in front of the other.

Think of determination as the fuel in your car's tank. Without it, you're not going anywhere. You can have the fanciest car, the best GPS, and a perfectly planned route, but without fuel, you're stuck. Determination keeps your engine running, propelling you forward, no matter how far you must go or how rough the road gets.

Persistence is like a gardener tending to their plants. It requires daily attention, watering, and weeding. Each day might not show dramatic results, but over time, those small efforts yield a lush, thriving garden. Your goals are like those plants—nurture them with consistent effort, and they'll grow into something beautiful.

Imagine your goals as a sculptor's block of marble. Persistence is the chisel that chips away at the stone, revealing the masterpiece within. Each strike might seem small, but it's essential. Without persistence, the sculpture remains hidden, trapped within the marble. But with steady, determined effort, you unveil the work of art that was always there.

Determination is like a lighthouse in the storm. It stands tall and unwavering, guiding you through the darkest nights and roughest seas. When you're tossed about by the waves of doubt and fear, determination provides a beacon of hope, showing you the way forward. It's your steady light in the storm of life.

Let us dive into the world of sports for a moment. Think about your favorite athlete—what sets them apart is not just talent but persistence and determination. They train every day, pushing through pain and fatigue, honing their skills with relentless focus. It is that unwavering commitment that leads to victory. So, channel your inner athlete and keep training for your personal gold medal.

Persistence is like a software update for your mind. It fixes bugs, improves performance, and adds new features over time. Each slight improvement might not seem like much, but collectively, they transform you into a more resilient, capable version of yourself. So, keep hitting that update button and watch yourself evolve.

Think of determination as a bulldozer clearing a path through a dense forest. It is powerful, relentless, and unstoppable. When you encounter obstacles,  determination does not just ask nicely for them to move—it powers through, pushing aside anything in its way. So, fire up your internal bulldozer and start clearing your path to success.

Persistence is the secret ingredient in grandma's famous recipe. It's what gives her cookies that extra bit of magic. She didn't perfect her recipe overnight—it took countless batches, many burnt edges, and a mountain of flour. But with each attempt, she got closer to perfection. So, when you are working towards your goals, remember that each effort, each tweak, brings you closer to your own sweet success.

Determination is like a GPS with a relentless attitude. It doesn't matter how many wrong turns you take or how often you end up on a detour—it recalculates and keeps you heading towards your destination. It might tell you to make a U-turn or take an unexpected route, but it never stops guiding you forward. Trust your internal GPS and keep moving, no matter how many recalculations it takes.

Imagine persistence as a game of fetch with an overenthusiastic dog. No matter how many times you throw the ball, that dog returns with it, tail wagging and ready for more. Life throws challenges, but like that dog, you keep returning the ball, eager for the next round. Each fetch gets you closer to mastering the game.

Determination is like planting a flag on the moon. It is a bold statement of your intent, that you are here to stay. It might take a rocket ship of effort to get there, and the journey might be fraught with challenges, but once you plant that flag, you have claimed your achievement. So, aim for the moon, and let determination be your rocket fuel.

Think of persistence as a marathon, not a sprint. It is about pacing yourself, keeping a steady rhythm, and pushing through the wall when your legs feel like jelly. Every mile marker is a testament to your endurance, and every step forward is a victory. So, lace up those running shoes and keep moving, one mile at a time.

Persistence is like tuning a guitar. Each adjustment might seem minor, but together, they create harmony. At first, you might struggle with dissonance, but with each tweak, you get closer to that perfect chord. Keep tuning your efforts, and soon, you'll play the melody of success.

Imagine determination as a loyal sidekick in your superhero journey. It's the Robin to your Batman, always by your side, ready to jump into action. No matter how tough the villains of doubt and fear are, your sidekick determination has your back, and you are prepared to fight for your dreams. Together, you are an unbeatable team.

Think of persistence as the glue that holds together the mosaic of your dreams. Each piece, no matter how small, is essential. Without persistence, the pieces would scatter, leaving your vision incomplete. But with it, you create a cohesive, beautiful picture that displays your dedication and hard work.

Determination is like a finely tuned engine. It provides the power and drive needed to keep moving forward. Each part, from the most miniature spark plug to the most enormous piston, works harmoniously to propel you towards your goals. Keep your determination engine well-maintained, and you'll easily reach your destination.

Persistence is like mastering a magic trick. It takes practice, patience, and a bit of trial and error. At first, you might fumble, but with each attempt, you get closer to pulling off the perfect illusion. And when you finally succeed, the applause is more rewarding, knowing you've earned it through sheer determination.

Determination is the foundation of a strong fortress. It provides stability and resilience, protecting you from doubts and setbacks. Each brick of effort adds to your fortress, creating a haven for your dreams. Keep building, and soon, you'll have an unshakable stronghold of success.

Persistence is like trying to solve a complex riddle. It requires patience, creativity, and a willingness to try different solutions. Each wrong answer brings you closer to the right one, sharpening your mind and honing your skills. Keep puzzling away, and you'll eventually crack the code.

Think of determination as the wind in your sails. It propels you forward, even when the waters are calm, or the storm clouds gather. With determination, you harness the power of the wind, navigating towards your goals with confidence and speed. So set your sails and let determination guide you to success.

Persistence is like a sculptor chiseling away at a block of marble. Each strike might seem small, but it's essential. Without persistence, the sculpture remains hidden, trapped within the marble. But with steady, determined effort, you unveil the work of art that was always there.

Finally, persistence and determination are the dynamic duo that can conquer any challenge. They are the keys to unlocking your potential, the secret weapons in your arsenal of success. Embrace them, nurture them, and let them guide you on your journey. With persistence and determination, there's no limit to what you can achieve. Thank you.

Ladies and gentlemen, fellow dream chasers, let's dive even deeper into the vast ocean of persistence and determination. Think of these two qualities as your life raft and paddle. The waves of life may try to swamp you, but with persistence, you stay afloat, and with determination, you paddle towards your goals, no matter how distant they may seem.

Persistence is your personal inner child. Remember how relentless kids are when they want something? "Can I have a cookie?" They ask again and again, unwavering, until you finally give in. That's the spirit you need to channel—embrace your inner cookie monster and keep asking life for what you want, no matter how many times it says "no."

Imagine determination as your very own power source, like a solar panel. It absorbs the energy from every setback, every sunny day, and every storm, converting them into the power needed to move forward. With determination, you're always charged up and ready to take on the next challenge, no matter what the weather brings.

Persistence is like a trusty old dog. No matter how many times it gets turned away or ignored, it always comes back with a wagging tail and hopeful eyes. It doesn't get discouraged; it doesn't give up. That unwavering faith and loyalty to the goal makes persistence so powerful. Be that old dog—never stop wagging, never stop trying.

Think of determination as your secret stash of chocolate hidden away for emergencies. When life gets tough, you break out that determination, and suddenly things don't seem so bad. It's the little  boost you need to keep going, to remind yourself that no matter how rough things get, you've got the sweetness of success waiting for you.

Persistence can be compared to the process of making a pearl. An oyster faces irritation and discomfort, but over time, it turns that grain of sand into something precious. Your challenges are the grain sand; with persistence, you can turn them into your own pearls of wisdom and achievement.

Determination is your internal clock that never stops ticking. It keeps you on track, reminding you of your goals and pushing you to keep moving forward, even when you'd rather hit the snooze button on life. That relentless tick-tock of ambition keeps you from staying stagnant, propelling you towards progress.

Picture persistence as a mountain goat, nimble and unyielding, scaling the steepest cliffs with ease. It doesn't matter how treacherous the terrain; the goat keeps climbing, confident and sure-footed. Be the mountain goat of your dreams—leap over obstacles, scale new heights, and never be afraid to tackle the toughest challenges.

Determination is like a superhero cape—wear it proudly, and it gives you the confidence to face any villain that crosses your path. With your cape of determination, you feel invincible, ready to swoop in and save the day, one small victory at a time. So put on your cape and let your inner superhero shine.

Think of persistence as a dedicated chef perfecting a recipe. Each attempt might require adjustments—a pinch more salt here, a dash less sugar there—but with each iteration, the di will iterate each iteration. Your goals are like that recipe—keep tweaking, keep trying, and eventually, you'll create a masterpiece.

Persistence is your personal echo in the canyon of life. You shout your dreams into the vast expanse, and persistence ensures they echo back, reminding you that your voice matters and your goals are heard. Every echo confirms that your efforts are reverberating, creating ripples of impact.

Imagine determination as a lighthouse keeper in a storm. The keeper's job is to ensure the light never goes out, guiding ships safely to shore. Your goals are those ships, and determination is the keeper who tirelessly maintains the light, no matter how fierce the storm. Keep your light burning bright, and you'll always find your way.

Persistence can be likened to a marathoner's mindset. It's not about how fast you start but about maintaining a steady pace, pushing through the pain, and keeping your eyes on the finish line. Each mile marker is a testament to your endurance, each step a declaration of your unwavering commitment.

Determination is like a seed that grows into a mighty tree. It starts small, but with time, care, and persistence, it grows strong roots and branches that reach for the sky. No storm can uproot it; no drought can wither it. Your dreams are the seeds; let determination be the soil, water, and sunlight that nurtures them.

Think of persistence as a friendly tugboat guiding a massive ship into harbor. The ship might be slow to respond, but the tugboat doesn't give up. It nudges, pulls, and pushes until the ship is safely docked. Be the tugboat for your goals—keep guiding, keep pushing, and eventually, you'll steer them to success.

Persistence is your invisible cloak of resilience. It shields you from the arrows of doubt and the slings of setbacks. With it, you move through life's battles with confidence, knowing that no matter how many hits you take, you're protected by the strength of your resolve.

Determination is like a loyal sidekick in the story of your life. It's always there, encouraging  you, picking you up when you fall, and celebrating your victories. The unwavering support keeps you going, reminding you that you are never alone on your journey. Embrace your sidekick and keep moving forward together.

Imagine persistence as the practice of yoga. It is about flexibility, balance, and the ability to hold your ground even in the most challenging poses. Each stretch and breath bring you closer to mastering your mind and body. Your goals are the ultimate yoga pose—keep stretching and balance, and you'll achieve them.

Think of determination as your personal lighthouse in the fog of uncertainty. It cuts through the mist, illuminating the path ahead. When you're lost or unsure, determination provides the clarity and focus needed to navigate through the murkiness. Keep your lighthouse bright, and you'll always find your way home.

Persistence is like learning to ride a unicycle. At first, it's all falls and wobbles, but with practice and determination, you find your balance and start to glide. Each attempt brings you closer to mastery, and soon enough, you're riding with confidence, showing the world what true persistence looks like.

Determination is your inner blacksmith, forging the steel of your resolve in the fires of adversity. Each hammer strike, each moment of intense heat, strengthens your will, shaping you into a formidable force. Embrace the forge and let determination mold you into an unbreakable achiever.

Imagine persistence as a dogged detective on a mission to solve the mystery of your dreams. It sifts through clues, follows leads, and never gives up, no matter how many dead ends it encounters.

Each step, each discovery, brings you closer to cracking the case. Be the detective— relentlessly pursue your dreams until the mystery is solved.

Think of determination as the process of brewing the perfect cup of coffee. It takes the right beans, the perfect grind, and just the right amount of time and pressure. Each brew might need adjustments, but with persistence, you'll craft the ideal blend that fuels your ambitions. Keep grinding, keep brewing, and savor the taste of success.

Persistence is like a skilled archer aiming for the bullseye. Each shot requires focus, control, and the willingness to keep trying, even when you miss. Over time, your aim improves, and you hit your target more often. Keep drawing your bow, keep aiming true, and eventually, you'll hit the mark every time.

Determination is the sturdy scaffolding that supports the construction of your dreams. It provides the structure and stability needed to build something magnificent. Each beam, each  plank, adds to the strength of your creation. Keep building, keep reinforcing, and soon you'll have a skyscraper of success towering above the skyline of your aspirations.

In conclusion, persistence and determination are the dynamic duo that can conquer any challenge. They are the keys to unlocking your potential, the secret weapons in your arsenal of success. Embrace them, nurture them, and let them guide you on your journey. With persistence and determination, there's no limit to what you can achieve. Thank you.

Call to Action

As you close this book, I encourage you to act. Reflect on your goals, develop a clear plan, and commit to persisting through challenges. Surround yourself with supportive individuals, embrace continuous learning, and celebrate your progress. Let persistence be your guiding principle as you navigate your journey to success. Remember, you have canvassed the competition and achieve your goals. Stay persistent, stay determined, and let your journey begin.

In conclusion, persistence is the key to achieving your dreams and surpassing the competition. It is a powerful force that drives you forward, transforms challenges into opportunities, and turns aspirations  into reality. By embracing the principles and strategies outlined in this book, you can harness the power of persistence and achieve extraordinary success. The journey may be extended and challenging, but the rewards are immense. Stay persistent, stay focused, and let your determination guide your goals. Your future is bright, and your potential is limitless. Keep pushing forward, and let persistence be your path to greatness. (A Personal Guide to Being Persistent). THIS CONCLUDES "How To Blow Pass the Competition and Get to Your Goal in Life (A Personal Guide to Being Persistent)"

Check Out A Book Bundle From
Brian's Other Famous Titles
"How To Get Past The Gatekeepers and
Get To Your Goal In Life:
A Personal Guide to Being Persistent"

NOTES...

NOTES...

NOTES...

NOTES...

Bibliography

1. **Covey, Stephen R.** *The 7 Habits of Highly Effective People: Powerful Lessons in Personal Change*. Simon & Schuster, 1989.

2. **Hill, Napoleon.** *Think and Grow Rich*. The Ralston Society, 1937.

3. **Kiyosaki, Robert T.** *Rich Dad Poor Dad: What the Rich Teach Their Kids About Money That the Poor and Middle Class Do Not!*. Plata Publishing, 1997.

4. **Tracy, Brian.** *Goals!: How to Get Everything You Want Faster Than You Ever Thought Possible*. Berrett-Koehler Publishers, 2003.

5. **Sinek, Simon.** *Start with Why: How Great Leaders Inspire Everyone to Take Action*. Portfolio, 2009.

6. **Dweck, Carol S.** *Mindset: The New Psychology of Success*. Ballantine Books, 2006.

7. **Vaynerchuk, Gary.** *Crush It!: Why NOW Is the Time to Cash In on Your Passion*. HarperStudio, 2009.

8. **Cardone, Grant.** *The 10X Rule: The Only Difference Between Success and Failure*. Wiley, 2011.

9. **Ferriss, Timothy.** *The 4-Hour Workweek: Escape 9-5, Live Anywhere, and Join the New Rich*. Crown Publishing Group, 2007.

10. **Thiel, Peter.** *Zero to One: Notes on Startups, or How to Build the Future*. Crown Business, 2014.

11. **Collins, Jim.** *Good to Great: Why Some Companies Make the Leap... and Others Don't*. HarperBusiness, 2001.

12. **Schultz, Howard, and Joanne Gordon.** *Onward: How Starbucks Fought for Its Life without Losing Its Soul*. Rodale Books, 2011.

13. **Maxwell, John C.** *The 21 Irrefutable Laws of Leadership: Follow Them and People Will Follow You*. Thomas Nelson, 1998.

14. **Sincero, Jen.** *You Are a Badass at Making Money: Master the Mindset of Wealth*. Viking, 2017.

15. **Dalio, Ray.** *Principles: Life and Work*. Simon & Schuster, 2017.

www.ingramcontent.com/pod-product-compliance
Lightning Source LLC
Chambersburg PA
CBHW071931210526
45479CB00002B/639